Published and distributed by

ISLAND HERITAGE
P U B L I S H I N G

99-880 IWAENA STREET, AIEA, HAWAII 96701-3202
PHONE: (808) 487-7299 • FAX: (808) 488-2279
EMAIL: hawaii4u@pixi.com

ISBN #089610-044-8
First Edition, First Printing – 1998

Footloose the Mongoose
& The Jumping Flea

By Elaine Masters
Illustrated by Jeff Pagay

DEDICATION

To all the Hawaiian keiki (and any mongooses, too) who
are learning to play the 'ukulele.

Enjoy!

Footloose the Mongoose lived in a little house with
his mother and father in the bushes by the big, wide ocean.
Every day he scampered up the coconut trees.
He splashed in the cool ocean waves.
And he rolled in the sun-warmed grass that grew
outside his little house.

2

Sometimes he watched old Mrs. Honu
teach the little turtles how
to count shells.

But mostly, he just played. That's why his friends called him "Footloose."

"You really should clean up your room," his mother said when she stuck her head in the door.

"You really should learn some responsibility," his father said when he saw him playing all day.

But his friend, Shifty, understood all about Footloose. "He will learn to work when the time is right," said Shifty, giving Footloose a slap on the back.

Then one day, when Footloose was rolling
in the sun-warmed grass that grew outside their little house,
he found a very strange thing.
It was made of wood.
It was about as long as he was, counting his tail.
And it had four plastic strings stretched tightly all along its body.

"Hmmm," said Footloose.
"I've never seen such a strange-looking wooden thing."
He picked it up. Gently, he pulled on one string.

"PLING," went the string,
in a high voice.
"My," said Footloose,
"What an awesome noise."
Gently, he pulled on the next string.
"PLANG," went the string,
in a lower voice.

7

A little finch sat on a bush nearby. It began to sing.
Quickly, Footloose plucked the strings, following the bird's song.
He played the song, and then the bird sang the song again.
Footloose played. The bird sang. It was kind of a game.

Then, a red-headed cardinal flew down to the ground beside Footloose.
It began a different song. Footloose could imitate his song, too.
When Shifty came by, he was impressed.
"You have a natural talent, Footloose." he said.
"When you play those songs, it sounds just like the birds singing."

But when his mother looked in his room, she said, "You still didn't clean up your room."
And his father asked, "When are you going to learn some responsibility?"
Shifty whispered to his friend, "Let's go see old
Mrs. Honu. I bet she will like your music."

Down at the beach, the little turtles stopped counting shells and started counting the strings on the strange-looking wooden thing.

One. Two. Three. Four.

Then they tried to count the notes as Footloose played bird songs for them, but there were too many notes. They couldn't count that high.

"Such lovely music," said Mrs. Honu. "You have a natural talent, Footloose. I've never known anyone who learned to play an 'ukulele *(oo-koo-lay-lay)* so quickly."

"'Ukulele?" said Footloose. "Is that what this is?"

"Yes," said Mrs. Honu. "Once I heard a person play one of those things. He played many notes at once and it sounded very beautiful."

"Hmm," said Footloose. " I wonder how he did that?"

"I don't know," said Mrs. Honu. "But I don't advise getting too close to people to find out! When I burrow down in the sand, they don't see me, but if you got close to them, they would see your beady eyes and your furry body."

"Yes," said Footloose, shivering with fear. "People are huge. I'm sure they are BIG TROUBLE."

Back in his little house, Footloose said to himself, "Mrs. Honu called it an 'ukulele. She said the people played many notes at the same time. How interesting!"

He picked up the 'ukulele and strummed his finger across all the strings.

BRA-A-A-NG! It sounded awful.

"There must be more to it than this," he said. "I need to watch a person play an 'ukulele."

He crept out of his house just as the sun was going down over the ocean.

He scampered along the edge of the bushes.
Footloose was afraid of the dark. He wanted to turn around.
He wanted to go back home. "A mongoose shouldn't be out at night,"
he said to himself. "Everybody knows that."

But then he said, "I must find out how people make beautiful music. I must."
On through the dark night he scampered. Past the bushes. Out by the ocean.
A fire burned on the beach. Sitting and talking around the fire were –

PEOPLE!

Footloose the Mongoose stopped, still.
He flattened himself down on the sand.
His beady little eyes darted from one person to another.
His muscles tensed in his wiry legs, ready to run away.

And then he heard it.
It was the same PLING-PLANG sound that his own 'ukulele made.
But it was several notes at once. And it was beautiful.
Where was it coming from? He had to find out.
His eyes darted back and forth.
And then he saw it.
Leaning against a log were a man and a little girl.
And in the girl's hands was –

an 'ukulele!

Inch by inch, keeping his body flat
against the sand, Footloose crept closer.
The man was showing the little girl where to put
her fingers on the strings.
"Like this," he said, moving her finger
to the next string. "Now, play."
The little girl strummed a finger
across the strings.

The little girl strummed a finger across the strings.
"That's it," the man encouraged her. "Good chord."

Then he took back the 'ukulele
and began to play.
Faster and faster his fingers
flew, until they looked like
jumping fleas.

Footloose was enchanted.
He forgot to be afraid.
He crept closer and closer, his eyes focused on
the man's flying fingers. The man pressed his
left-hand fingers down on the strings while his
right hand strummed the rhythm.

22

"Ah!" said Footloose. "So THAT'S how they do it!"

Suddenly—
"Look, a mongoose!" a boy shouted. He ran toward Footloose. Footloose froze.
Then, the muscles in his legs went into action.
He turned and fled. *ZIP!* He dashed back into the bushes.

WHOOSH! He raced through the shadows.

He rushed inside his little house and locked the door.
He panted a few moments, leaning against the locked door, and fanned himself.

Then he pulled out his 'ukulele.
He began to practice. He held down two or three strings with
the fingers on his left paw. He strummed with his right paw.
PL-I-NG. It sounded pretty good!

He tried some more chords.
He strummed and strummed. The more he
practiced, the better the chords sounded.
He practiced all night. His paws grew tired. He got blisters on his fingers.
He worked very hard, but he was having so much fun, it didn't seem like work.

In the morning, Shifty came to visit.
"What beautiful music!" he exclaimed.
"How did you learn to do that?"

"I learned it from watching people," said Footloose.

"What?" Shifty exclaimed.

"Yes," said Footloose. "People are big and scary looking, but I had to find out about those chords. And now, I've practiced and practiced, and – well, just listen."

"PL-I-NG, PL-A-NG." Footloose played the most beautiful music Shifty had ever heard.

Now, Footloose the Mongoose is much in demand for concerts.

He plays for the turtle lūʻaus. He plays for the bird recitals.

His father is very proud that his son has learned responsibility.
But his mother still wishes he would clean up his room.

IN CASE YOU'RE WONDERING

The mongoose was deliberately brought to Hawai'i many years ago to get rid of rats. However, a rat is active at night and a mongoose is active in the day. They seldom meet!

The 'ukulele was brought to Hawai'i by the Portuguese before 1900. When Hawaiians saw it, they called it an "'ukulele" (say *oo-koo-lay-lay*, pronouncing the "u" like the "oo" in "mongoose"). In the Hawaiian language, the word really means "jumping flea" (uku = flea, lele = jump). The player's fingers moved so quickly that it reminded the Hawaiians of jumping fleas.

Hawaiians call the mongoose a "manakuke" (say *mah-nah-koo-kay*) since there is no "g" or "s" in the Hawaiian alphabet.

Usually, a mongoose does not play an 'ukulele. Footloose did, indeed, have a natural talent.

THE END